Bites Of Insanity

Nsah Mala

Langaa Research & Publishing CIG
Mankon, Bamenda

Publisher:
Langaa RPCIG
Langaa Research & Publishing Common Initiative Group
P.O. Box 902 Mankon
Bamenda
North West Region
Cameroon
Langaagrp@gmail.com
www.langaa-rpcig.net

Distributed in and outside N. America by African Books Collective
orders@africanbookscollective.com
www.africanbookscollective.com

ISBN: 9956-792-67-5

© Kenneth Toah Nsah (Nsah Mala) 2015

Foreword

Bites of Insanity is a brilliantly written collection of fifty seven poems which represent psycho-somatic, psycho-social and ecological degradation characteristic of the poet's society. The interdisciplinary and intertexual nature of the collection is impressive. The poems are very rich in imagery as they convey disillusionment, bitterness and the general trauma in which youths and the entire population of Cameroon and elsewhere have been plunged by irresponsive and deadened governmental and gruesome political machineries. The collection presents issues bordering on state politics, the prevalence of malaria both as pathology and metaphor, the vain nature of power, the Anglophone Problem, and optimism when faced with human woes. The collection addresses other issues like hotspots on the globe with regard to crises of international concern, carnage, nationalism, deontology in higher education, ethical problems on almost all spheres of life, dangerous friendships, and ecological awareness and sustainability.

The strength of the collection lies in the multifaceted perspectives with which insanity from a national, continental and intercontinental can be construed. The poems are highly pregnant and suggestive. Insanity in the population results from the insanity of manned historical, social, economic and political forces which are completely out of tune. Morality and decency appear to have been extinguished where they have to flourish. Kleptomania, tribalism, nepotism, wanton embezzlement, undemocratic and excessively bad governance are practices which are asphyxiating the populace and transforming many into lunatics or subhuman beings.

Insanity collocates with absurdity, irrationality, senselessness, folly and madness; these terms give a vivid picture of progressively regressing modern societies.

Nsah Mala wrestles with a system which could best be construed as entrenched in what Michel Foucault and Achille Mbembe have respectively described as bio-power/politics and necropolitics. Values have radically been inverted: What is senseless should be conceived as what makes sense; what is enigmatic is what should be comprehensible; what is irrational is what should be rational and acceptable; what is amoral unproblematically takes precedence over the moral. In fact, the defence mechanism of rationalization characteristic of most states has set the pace with which to understand loud sounding rhetoric and political magniloquence. The health sector is a sad story when one looks at the deeper undercurrents of cholera, typhoid and mosquito related pathologies; particularly cerebral malaria (finely represented in 'Bites of Insanity'), which to the poet's conviction, are politically motivated. The body is politically used as site/space of ideological inscription, amplified by psychological quiescence which has annihilated any tint of human agency.

Nsah Mala is ascertaining his status as a committed social critic in very uncompromising terms. His contemptuousness of postcolonial states' ab/uses of power in the bastardisation of citizens/subjects is undoubted. The decadence and moral depravity in which a directionless nation finds herself are pointers of impending destruction unless the situation is redressed.

Nsah Mala makes a mockery of postcolonial autocrats who conceive of power as uniquely pertaining to a select group of cohorts and sycophants. Such misguided repressiv leaders never care about the unchallengeable naturalistic or deterministic law that power is not eternal but tragically ephemeral. Whether a military dictatorship or civilian dictator backed by the military, the outcomes are usually similar. 'After the Coup' presents a historical circumstance, in which the powerlessness of abusive power operates, affirming the delusion that personalisation/presidentialisation of power is destructive. The case of the former president of Central African Republic Francois Bozizé with whom the poem is concerned is not isolated in Africa and beyond, and reverberates in creative works such as Sony Labou Tansi's Shameful State, Asongwed Tah's Born to Rule and Nkemngong Nkengasong's Black Caps and Red Feathers. Bozizé snatched power through a coup d'état, was politically epileptic, orchestrated mass killings and bloodshed, and was shamefully ousted through the same mechanism and reduced to nothing. Blaise Campaoré's predicament is still fresh in the memory. The shock is that such unilateral exercises of Mephistophelean power, further exemplified in 'Dirt and Rubbish' in which even sycophants have become adversaries, only leads to chronic short-sightedness and irreparable tragedy either by death or brutal dispossession of power. The greatest tragedy about Africa is that such situations of complete dysfunction between state and society would be perpetual given the complex political dynamics of neo-colonialism and globalisation.

The international dimension of gross abuse of power is finely textualised in 'Syrian and Other Graveyards' where man's acclaimed sense of rationality is strongly interrogated and deconstructed. Senseless killings and wanton destruction of environment and property by "politico-economic drunks" with the complacency of some super powers/permanent members of the UN Security Council, is uncontested manifestation of the incurability of human insanity. The images of countless corpses, some mutilated by ballistic weapons, the site of bombed or butchered women and innocent children without any opportunity of right of burial convey what critics like Susan Sontag and Zoe Norridge respectively analyse in Regarding the Pain of Others and Perceiving Pain in African Literature.

This exposure of human corpses is inviting to mean creatures which are personified as ridiculing humanity's debasing nature and:

> mocking man's inhumanity to man
> and celebrating
> this sudden twist of values—
> the beastification of humans and
> the humanisation of beasts

This despicable human tragedy is recurrent in Syria, Libya, Ukraine, Nigeria, and many other unnamed spots of the world. The poem is also subtly contemptuous of the double edged sword United Nations which is not doing much to better humanity's destiny in face of manmade and natural calamities.

'Eclipsed Family Name', 'Family Farm' and 'Sometimes I Wonder' usher another trajectory of discourse of manipulation of power in the postcolony. The poems are a veiled statement of the Cameroon Anglophone Problem to which Nsah Mala cannot possibly be indifferent. Following the tradition of established Anglophone authors such a Victor Epie Ngome, Bole Butake, Bate Besong, Nkemngor Nkengasong, Alobwed'Epie, John Ngong Kum Ngong a

Nol Alembong, Nsah Mala's aestheticises the problem through a series of metaphors bordering on diverse aspects of family. As a historiographer he makes known his positionality with regard to the Anglophone-Francophone polarities in the country where the state professes unity and indivisibility as trademarks. Two blood brothers were ideological demarcated in what one would call a game of Western giants:

Our sun-baked-skin parents
compelled and compacted us
into two toiling brother blocks
namedCambo and Camfo
after a family chat beyond the seas.

We started grumbling, grumbling,
grumbling like caged lions for our freedom.
Uncle Everybody scolded our parents
who escaped into dark hiding holes
and telewooed us into an incestuous union.

These lines and imagery relate to the context in which colonialism and neo-colonialism have manipulated and torn Africans apart as the clash is more of contestations of Western legacies rather than ethno-centred political realities.

In the second poem Nsah Mala laments the servitude on which one of two supposedly equal partners is enmeshed and condemned. Farm and unequal division of labour and profit parallel the estate we encounter in Bole Butake's Family Saga where Kamala and Kamalo are at strife because of ncompatible colonial legacies and a huge misunderstanding their common ancestral/mythic heritage.

Nsah Mala's poetic style is unique; simple but insightful. In 'Musical Madness' Nsah Mala's imaging of immorality and indecency is fascinating. Music has ceased to serve a social function and is reduced to pleasures of the flesh which bear absolutely no relevance to societal advancement or redemption:

With dancers dressed half naked
We see chest-melons rise and fall
　　While dancers vibrate
Like erupting, angry Mount Fako
And sway heads left and right
　　Like mad lizards
Male onlookers wet inner wears
In extreme excitement while
　　Bikutsi and Makossa
Lure feeble fellows and fools
Into new Sodoms and Gomorrahs
　　Beastifying Mankind forever.

These lines finely express the amoral dangers which have gripped the fabric of our postmodernist society. Anarchy and carnal laissez-faire are watchwords while the erosion of valued cultural practices is of no concern. Nsah Mala laments cultural/moral deracination in uncompromising terms. 'Crying Fons' paints this sad image of traditional rulers who have ceased to be vanguards of cultures and are now desecrators of culture in pursuit of selfish modern political ends; they have simply joined the bandwagon of political gangsters whose focus is nothing but their narcissistic self. Social rottenness is viral and has negatively affected the enti system in 'Hygiene Corruption'. In 'The Bank of Secre moral wilderness and hollowness are represented in diverse spaces and mentalities which interact within such spaces. Survival of the fittest is all that remains of a society which is completely abandoned by an absurd and absent-minded governmental system which curiously passes for a messianic instrument to the wretched populace.

A poem like 'Writing Feyiyn's Wrongs' hinges on the social ulcer known as prostitution, especially as it involves conscious reorientation of the body for the pleasure principle. The intellectual twist in the poem is man's attempt to deconstruct God's work on his physiognomy. In fact, the wrongs of God are righted by overzealous women who aim at artificializing their bodies in the name of beauty and attraction for capitalist gains.

> Feyiyn was blind to beautify brows with hair
> Feyiyn was brainless to make breasts for babies
> Feyiyn was dull to dress Eve below knees
> Feyiyn was foolish to make feet flat
> Woman is right to shave brows and advertise breasts
> Woman is right to be nude on very high heels
>
> These women are righting Feyiyn's wrongs
> And multiplying His wrath by more wrongs

Feyiyn is divine creator whose creation has been transgressed by humanity's vaulting ambition. Society seems to be in the terminal phase of a protracted pathology. This same phenomenon finds expression in 'Hovering Around Yaoundé' where the artificialisation of God's work is part of the cyber culture of attracting carnal/material interest leading curious marriages:

Half-nude damsels
with reddened lips and
hyper-bleached visages
in the company of lazy crazy
westernized boys make nuptial
plans in electronic madness.

An informed reader cannot be indifferent to the socio-economic and political variables which have orchestrated such moral malaise and taking of a wrong turn.

'Blood Banks' represents a dual image; the mosquito as insect which does not only suck blood but injects sickly bacteria into the human system, and the political zombie wearing human face, but literally sucking the populace dry of its essence. In other terms mosquitoes are a metaphor for socio-political oppressors who have dehumanized the helpless for their self-centred ends. The poem therefore suggests the zombification of a system at the mercy of an autocrat and his sycophants.

'Mimboman' depicts part of Yaounde's cityscape as a derelict moral wasteland not different from a mortuary as the poet evinces. Mimboman is a dead end, a space which has faded in a miasma of despair and hopelessness, anarchy and mystery. Describing Yaounde as "treacherous" calls for no doubt as it is a city rife with insecurity and utter uncertainty. The corpse depicts not only the lifelessness of the mutilated and abandoned victim; it is by extension a representation of the capital city which has always been described as the heart or life wire of the nation but somewhat deadened in its inner core. Nsah Mala reiterates:

Here is both mortuary and grave

Yawning wounds conspicuously
Sit where breasts and genitals
Stood when this victim was alive

Perhaps, some drugged riff-raffs
Drugged him or her in darkness
To get fresh flesh for some rites
To propel some white-coated boss into power

These stanzas convey a strong sense of awfulness regarding this emblematic landscape. The last stanza particularly wrestles with a very disturbing phenomenon in the insanity characteristic of material and power quest in the Cameroonian society. Occult practices are increasingly rampant and associated with the corridors of state power and materialist obsessions. Human sacrifice is part of the demonic logic of having appointments and exercising control over the weak majority and innocent. In 'Head in a Bag' Nsah Mala reiterates disgust of how an insane society operates with regard to inhuman quest for financial aggrandisement through devilish sacrifice of human body parts.

With regard to ecocritical paradigms Nsah Mala celebrates ecological grandeur and sustainability in a poem like 'Leaves on Leave', but most disturbingly, Nsah Mala bitterly denounces eco-unfriendliness resulting from man's heartless devastation of fauna and flora and the ozone layer. 'Environmental Foes', 'Innocent Ozone', 'Shrubs' Emergency', 'Hovering Above Yaoundé' and 'Mokolo Slums' image different ways in which neglect of environment is retrogressively impacting lives. 'Environmental Foes' portrays man as wreaking havoc on nature and environment:

At daggers drawn we are
nature's foes mingle and dine
with us like Judas while
they ready to kidnap trees
and assassinate fauna and
betray themselves ignorantly
who are enemies of Environment?

The ending question is a rhetorical question because one needs not imagine that the environment can be self-destructive. The infringing external disruptor of nature's essence is man.

'Hovering Above Yaoundé' reverberates the physical and psychological landscape in T S Eliot's 'The Love Song of J Alfred Prufrock' and 'The Waste Land':

Rusty serpentine roads
meander through yawning
heaps of frightening garbage
depicting
a people of lost values,
a people of dead hygiene.

Cholera's sirens
echo and re-echo across
the protruding
walls of cherished garbage
and stagnant germ pounds,
healing filth-ridden residents
and whispering benedictions
of nausea.

The stench and pollution signal ill health and generate indescribable existentialist unease. Nsah Mala goes further to relate the dysfunction between man and environment, using vivid images of filth, decay, nausea and sickness:

Humans and dirt are
bedfellows; bugs and
caterpillars are witnesses
to all acts on
matrimonial beds.
Banana and cane peelings
are tiles;
plastic bags and rags
are carpets
while tincans and used-lotion bottles
are alarm clocks.
Dirtiness is acquired
alongside mother tongues
since dust bins and garbage cans
are too expensive to procure
and HYZACAM is never near enough…

Good sanitary conditions are farfetched in the surroundings painted in these lines. HYZACAM stands for the company that is responsible for collection and disposal of garbage in Yaounde. It is overwhelmed by its incapacity to accurately perform its duty toward the environment. Created since 1969 the company today appears to by a mere relic of its one time commitment to environmental sanity. Presently it can cater only for certain portions of the city while the rest survives in the darkness of decay. Ecological degradation is depicted in a cityscape 'Mokolo Slums' which has lost consciousness of healthy environment and its benefits to all spheres of life…swampy slums and squalors, horrible marshlands as habitats with the implicating health disasters like cholera, typhoid and malaria are environmental tradition.

Amidst gloom and bleakness the poet does not sound pessimistic and discouraging. 'I Have Hope' sounds a note of optimism amidst the poet's apprehension of the bleakness of society. In this particular poem Nsah Mala uses the pronoun 'I' from a personalist perspective. There is no doubt that the poem is a veiled confession of his victimhood in the system. But he is self-conscious of his ability to alter things and make a difference.

'Make Sounds for Pounds' communicates a pro-Sartrean existentialist conviction that man can determine the circumstances of his life if he engages himself in a productive action. Man, according to Nsah Mala, has the freewill or volition to struggle to give meaning to his life. As an agent man should not lazy around when he possesses the innate capacity to make worthwhile choices for his existential fulfilment. One important issue discernible from the poem is man's polyvalent nature; he has many talents which can be exploited. Every genuine effort sooner or later would be fruitful, but docility is the brainchild of inertia.

The poems convincingly address salient current issues in contemporary Cameroon, postcolonial Africa and the world at large. The depth of discourse is all the same not determined by the numerical strength of the collection, but the multitude of debates it inspires. *Bites of Insanity* is not so much about the devastation of the malaria epidemic as it is about subtle human mosquitoes in political spheres. It embraces a manifold of phenomena which showcase the woes of human existence. A review would certainly not do theoretical and critical justice to the intrinsic and extrinsic interpretive fertility of the poems. The poems are therefore rich in contents and aesthetics, and are highly recommended to any reader in African literary, social and political studies.

Charles Ngiewih Teke
University of Munich, 2014

When the poet philosophizes and advises...

Forbidden

Hello, my Reader!
Drop me not down
Once you've begun to drown
Your reading tentacles into me, reader.
These verses you read
Are my skeleton wrought with a reed,
A hollow reed which stains
The world with words and strains
To anchor wisdom to hearts
Like Cupid anchoring love to hearts.
Divorce me not and turn
Not to liquor bottles to dissolve
Reason; rather resolve
With me to grasp the Crown in turn
When silent chances sail slowly
And at lightning speed, but surely,
Into our impatient dragnets
While we browse internets
Of prayers and chant them upwards
And espouse the Lamb to leap forwards.

(Mbankolo, 30 November 2012)

I Have Hope

I have hope
That one day
These baggy, tar-eaten shoes
On my long walking tyres
Shall give way
To golden, well-polished Syrian shoes.
It may be there
Beyond the skies.
It may be here
Below the skies.

I have hope
That one day
These tattered, yawning ancient clothes
On my underfed skeletal chassis
Shall give way
To sparkling, white African Danchikis.
It may be there
Beyond the skies.
It may be here
Below the skies.

I have hope
That one day
These naked, barren, overnight meals
On my bamboo, termite-eaten dining tables
Shall give way
To spicy, jocund, well-stewed porridges.
It may be there
Beyond the skies.

It may be here
Below the skies.

I have hope
That one day
These crosses of fasting, suffering and poverty
On my weak, weak human shoulders
Shall give way
To interminable abundance, joy and dishes.
It may be there
Beyond the skies.
It may be here
Below the skies.

I have hope
That one day
These insults and prejudices our East-Mongolians
On us inflict over these Western waste borders
Shall give way
To freedom and smooth paths to the Crown.
It may be there
Beyond the skies.
It may be here
Below the skies.

(Monatélé II, 08 January 2013)

Hands and Mouth

The eyes can see.
The ears can hear.
But unless the mouth talks,
There is no trouble.

The heart can feel.
The mind can conceive.
But unless the mouth speaks,
There is no trouble.

The heart can nurse jealousy.
The mind can plan evil.
But unless the hands act,
There is no trouble.

Eyes and ears are inlets,
But hands and mouth are outlets:
They are outlets of trouble,
The trouble that ruins the body…

(Monatélé II, 15 March 2013)

Best Friend

Real friends I thought we were
Because I lent him my whole heart
And trusted him like Rabbi did Iscariot where
We know—Iscariot's was a heartless heart!
The doors of my within
For him I left ajar,
Letting collapse the walls of doubt within;
Unaware that from afar,
He rushed into my life
To tread on my soul
And switch me off alive

And celebrate divorce for my body & soul.
Tender invitations to alehouses
He would offer me
And we'd brave mud and rains into victual houses
For last supers, though unknown to me.
My hook he baited with money
And decorated my dragnet with words.
And I never knew all these were all phoney
Until Feyiyn sent me warning words.
That's how they usually come,
These murderous friends who
Like butchers caress you to come
To their abattoir. They, who
Lured you into this abattoir, kill
You mercilessly for their food.
Now I know this fiend wants to kill
Me out of jealousy for his food.
friend he is
t, but a fiend he is.

5

Into his snares he will tumble
Himself, but I cannot tumble
There 'cause Feyiyn is my Shepherd.

(Mbankolo, 12 October 2012)

The Old Testament

Our Prophets' Old
Testament may be very old
in name, but never in value.

(Mbankolo, 22 August 2012)

What's Man?

    Man's but
chunks of perishable
    flesh
    glued on
immortal glossy bones,
    caging
a mysteriously
immortal breath,
    gullibly
awaiting Death
    who
    inevitably
    sacrifices him
to termites and maggots,
to scavengers and ants,
to beetles and vultures.

When alive,
    Man
takes up many different
shapes, sizes,
colours and heights
    and
like a giraffe
may brag about
ephemeral beauty
and wealth
until Death
waylays him
and exiles him
down

to the Land of his
unique universal
skeletal form.

Man's
nothing but
a lifeless skeleton
          with
everlastingly laughing,
          friendly
and shinning teeth.

(Mbankolo, 18 August 2012)

Sometimes I Wonder

(From personal experience and that of Ndikechu Greg.)

Sometimes I wonder whether
the Soa-Ngoa rectors
know this:
that in computer central units,
students' marks
are swapped
for coins, for wads, for sex and for tribes;
that students' results
walk away
'never to return'
like Head's Elizabeth;
that some offices
on campus are brothels…

Sometimes I wonder whether
wind can't
inform ministers of this:
that innocent files
have aged to death point
in callous drawers
in some ministerial offices
because their owners
either
did not dissect wallets
or
were accidentally born
to babble
the Queen's Tongue
or turned down fondling invitations…

Sometimes I wonder whether
the powers that be
know this:
that some of these less-brains
who flood our professional schools
divorced from merit
and got married to
money migration
before punishing these tired desks;
that names were murdered
from among final lists
on their way
to billboards…

Sometimes I wonder whether
the mute statues in church
can't inform priests of this:
that these front-seat black suits
and white gowns
who change cars like
a chameleon changes colours
raise and swing
their hands too
in Lucifer's assemblies;
that God frowns at priests
who create artificial scarcity
of Holy Water,
making it a luxury
reserved only for generous thieves
 and greedy neighbours
who dance up for second and third offertory baskets.
(Mbankolo, 16 August 2012)

Never

say come and take
to your baby
because next time
 s/he won't budge
if there is no gift.

exploit your husband
and run away
because your next husband
will prey on you
and your ill-gotten wealth.

woo a maiden
by displaying your wealth
because she'll quit you
when misery
knocks at your doors.

sound joyous trumpets over
your enemy's death
because friends too
do die since
death spares nobody.

say you will die
and see to anybody
because death doesn't
 have friends;
death spares nobody.

maltreat and misuse
an orphan in your keeping
because orphanhood
is not a choice; your
children's case will be worst.

grow crops of jealousy
on your friend's/neighbour's farm
because a Supreme Eye
sees you and Divine Hands
will water your farms with acidic rains.

say I'm more intelligent
than you to anybody
because knowledge is unevenly
spread like natural resources
and you never can access/assess others' brains.

(Mbankolo, Sunday 5 August 2012, while on my sick bed,
suffering from malaria)

I Am An Orphan

(For All Who Care about Orphans throughout the World)

I am an orphan.
My parents slipped off my hands
Into the endless bliss of other lands,
Leaving me an orphan.

I am an orphan.
I just lost two droplets of parents.
Now I swim in endless oceans of parents
Who treat me as an orphan.

I am an orphan.
I am God's measuring rode of care.
This God whose judgment is fair
Made me an orphan.

I am an orphan.
I am God's love-barometer
And His charity-thermometer
Since He made me an orphan.

I am an orphan.
Our orphanage is God's consulate on earth
Which issues visas to paradise from earth.
So He made me an orphan.

I am an orphan.
God uses me in His judgment

But I cannot escape His judgment
Just because I am an orphan.

I am an orphan.
I shouldn't be a lake without outlets,
Swallowing and swelling without outlets
Just because I am an orphan.

I am an orphan.
I must spread love and care to others
And practice sharing with others
Because everybody is an orphan.

(Obala, Sunday February 02, 2014)

After The Coup

(Following Francois Bozize's Overthrow in March 2013)

Before the coup,
He was always right
In his gun-point might.
When he shouted like thunder,
We, in slum-huts, had to chunder
In fear of venomous grenades and bullets.
But today he is without amulets,
After the bloody coup.

Before the coup,
Bozize was the hard rock
And could carelessly mock
Us behind dark-glassed limousines
When escorted to cut-throat French cuisines.
Limousines in long, long queues
No longer parade him in these curfews
After the bloody coup.

Before the coup,
He made countless flights,
Leaving us without lights.
He owned and ruled the state,
And we were the state.
An earlier coup gave him this mission,
But now he cannot even rule a subdivision

After the bloody coup.

Before the coup,
Bozize was king of elephants,
Trampling us like road-ants,
While impregnating his wallets.
He pitilessly used us like mallets,
But today he has lost the game
And has crumbled till we're all the same
After the bloody coup.

(Mbankolo, 27 March 2013)

Termites And Birds

What happens
when winged termites
become wingless
after the morning rain?
Only hungry fowls
and birds can tell.

What happens
when free West-Mongolians
become bounded slaves
after the Foumban downpour?
Only hollow-stomached Betis
and East-Mongolians can tell.

What happens
when grazing antelopes
get entangled in nets
after belled-dogs bark?
Only roaring-stomached hunters
and smoke-darkened pots can tell.

What happens
when Victoria's kids
become orphans and beggars
after crossing the Adhi-Ngu Hammock?
Only Louis' bastard lice
and frogs can tell.

What happens
when mating rats
become fatty food

after sliding on python-spittle?
Only long, dark intestines
and anterior holes can tell.

What happens
when sane slum-dwellers
become drunken merry-men
after the hilarious campaign toast?
Only prefilled ballot boxes
and double votes/counts can tell.

(Mbankolo, 16 March 2013)

Cloudy Day

(In memory of a terrible day in my life, November 15, 2012)

1.
The Horizons open wide eyes
To peep on Earth.
Hunger's sons and daughters
Hit hard on my stomach's doors.
Then orphaned fried egg
And yellowish naked
Cassava powder (garri),
Baptized in hot Jordan,
Bid them welcome.

2.
Another clouded-sunny day is born.
To Nlongkak Governor's Office
I leap lousily and doubtfully,
With borrowed smiles
On my face sprayed
To conceal distrust.

3.
Rivers of cloudy file-chasers
Flood and flood the place,
Firing Ewondo verbal squads
Into my rioting mind and ears,
Reminding me to trust none
In this thorny battlefield
Where every smile
Sheds layers of distrust
And dishonesty

And fraud
And famine
And decay
And disgust.

4.

Yet Tanyitiku Egbe implants
Her roots of confidence
Into these sandy soils
And disagrees to agree
With me that the Kamerun desert
Is void of trust oases
And full of oceans of deceit.

5.

After aeons of hopeless waiting,
The clouded medical booklets
Cruise into our fatigued palms.
These medical booklets,
These medical booklets,
Struggling under
Conspicuous and suspicious
Signatures and stamps
From ghost renowned medics,
To declare our aptitude
 To serve the State.

6.

Medical booklets?
Yes, medial booklets,
 But never ask
  nd put to task

The stethoscopes
And microscopes
That examined us
Because they all died
In the next
Clinical operation....

7.
My heart and mind clad in Thomas suits,
I brave hot and menacing solar spears.
Then I vamoose into ENS Yaoundé's
Département de Français of fears,
Knock and knock and knock like an Angel,
But no answer emerges from within.
Then unawares I take her
Like Palestinians to Israelis did on Yom Kimpur.
Her lips and teeth are at work,
Busily burying a loaf of bread.
"Monsieur Fouda vient de sortir"
Answers my gentle request
For my own transcript
Whose application letter
Has for three weeks
Been dancing one tune here:
"Monsieur Fouda n'est pas là".

8.
Like a serpent which has swallowed a rat,
I drag along my heavy self to Ngoa-Ekelle
For another transcript of mine.
Indeed even frustration is graded!

9.

Not only do I knock on Scolarité door
As if on a mortuary door,
but there my eyes are cursed to see
An adult woman wailing like a waterfall
In this deaf and dumb office
After all her efforts to get a BA testimonial
Have been shattered and scattered by
Franco-frustration and flung
Down the cliffs of surrender
Where death watches
All victims through
Suicidal lenses…

10.

"Enough is enough,"
I resolve in me,
Deep, deep down in me
And haste homewards
Ready to break the barracks
Of Kamerun like Takwi
When time and God
Join my cleansing team.

(Mbankolo, 16 November 2012)

Kfifoyn's Verdicts

"Money for Mbeh's Bird
I never stole for sure,"
Maraba's defense in case of Bird.
His heart and mind are pure.

"Together with Mbeh's assistants,
Maraba, you stole village wealth,"
Retorts Chief Judge's assistants.
Their Fon's Bird was from our wealth.

In a lightless, roadless, houseless village,
A Fon intends to misuse village coins
To procure a golden Bird not for village
But for himself; and yet with general coins.

"Make sure Maraba is jailed,"
Mbeh to Kfifoyn's Chief Judge on telephone.
Anyone who eyes his Crown must be jailed.
He needs only hint Kfifoyn on telephone.

"Your will be done, Mbeh,"
Chief Judge replies in trembling voice.
Since he was chosen by Mbeh,
The truth he can never ever voice.

To serve Mbeh well one has
To divorce with good conscience
And always obey like a toy one has
And learn to excel in occultist science.

"Though you served Mbeh, Maraba,
You are now a thief guilty of treason,"
Kfifoyn's Chief Judge tells Maraba
And his ruling is full of reason.

"Thirty years of repentance
For you, Maraba, in darkness.
No one can come to your assistance.
So your plans will wither in darkness."

Thus Maraba and likes are imprisoned.
Back at home Chief Judge cannot sleep.
What rest with a conscience imprisoned?
He wrestles with bed sheets in vain to sleep.

(Mbankolo, 22 December 2012)

Family Farm

Our first Dad adopted us in 1919 abroad.
Twenty years afterwards, he was murdered abroad.
His death dust took six years to settle down abroad.
In 1945, his blood brother succeeded him abroad.

Our Dad's two wives all lived abroad.
Brigette, my Mom, was raising us while abroad.
Flavian, our half brothers' Mom, also lived abroad.
Our Moms later disowned us and joined Daddy abroad.

Our elder brothers held meetings here at home
And decided to merge our two farms here at home.
Mother Flavian advised her children here at home
To be wise in the family meetings held here at home.

My blood brothers went like orphans to the meetings
And were blindfolded to sell our farm in the meetings
To our half brothers who organised the meetings
That held along Noun's banks as family meetings.

Our two farms have become one family farm.
Whilst we toil like bees on our portion of the farm,
Our half brothers work like snails on their farm
And channel our crops and waters into their farm.

Our crops bear like April-tomatoes on the farm
And our half brothers' like January-figs on the farm.
For them, our fruits are on their own portion of the farm
Since they always connect them into baskets on their farm.

We wallow in misery while in serious slavery
On the farm; we are kept in serious slavery.
Our parents must help free us from the slavery
Before we use hammers to break the locks of slavery.

We must break up this farm into two farms
And live on the fruits of our own farms.
While Peace breezes, this farm should become farms
Before the heat of our anger melts rocks on the farms.

(Mbankolo, 03 September, 2013)

Eclipsed Family Name

We were blood brothers,
with one name: Kamun.
Then our foster stranger-parents
poured in like hailstones
after beating our Dad in a squabble.

Our sun-baked-skin parents
compelled and compacted us
into two toiling brother blocks
named Cambo and Camfo
after a family chat beyond the seas.

We started grumbling, grumbling,
grumbling like caged lions for our freedom.
Uncle Everybody scolded our parents
who escaped into dark hiding holes
and telewooed us into an incestuous union.

Like a bat, brother Camfo
has swallowed my name
and instead of vomiting Kamun
he has vomited Camfo
dragging our family name into an eclipse.

(Mbankolo, 26 August, 2013)

Kamerun's Flag

(Sunday 2nd September 2012. Dr Teke Charles has invited me to International Day celebrations in their church, Lighthouse Chapel International, Carrefour Scalom-Yaoundé. During flag parade phase of activities, my eyes begin to itch with tears as different national flags are paraded. When the Kamerun flag takes stage in the company of the Kamerun National Anthem, I irresistibly burst into tears of joy as usual.)

This tri-coloured piece of cloth
Connects me to Kamerun like
An umbilical cord connects foetus and mother. Cloth
Of green red yellow and star, I like
Thee. To hoist and hull thee down
Is a barometer for country love.
When birds chant melodious notes at dawn,
We chorus the Foulassi Song of love

And stand at attention to escort
Thee in the journey up
Thy staff in readiness to export
Our pacific ancestral cultures up
North to the World Market of Cultures.
Like our Fathers, we toil in peace
And love to invest in agriculture
To merit our name: Island of Peace.

When I wander across our frontiers,
This magical cloth magnetizes me home
As it triggers my glands of tears
Each time I see it. 'Come home',
In a deafening whisper, Mbamba's Anthem

Tells me and beckons me homeward.
Though we've murdered the Idea from Athens,
We must home and toil and love upward.

(Mbankolo, 3 August 2012

When the poet puts on traditional regalia and plays
ancestral music…

Crying Fons

Babysitters of customs and traditions
In yesteryears they were
These Fons who today cry
As their loose morals
Dye their dignity and
Wash away their worth and valor

Vanguards of cultures and peoples
In yesteryears they were
These Fons who now cry
As desecrated, furious Earth
Breeds healthy-conscience sons
To draw daggers and hark all desecrators

These Fons and Chiefs
Who in bygone centuries
Were crossroads of politics and religions
Now cry in shame
As they line behind bastard liars
Shaking hands and rubbing shoulders
With state burglars like
Children who misuse charms on their wrists

These Fons and Chiefs
Who in years gone by
Were loving Mothers
Spreading out tender arms

To welcome both black and white children
Now cry and chunter
As their dignity bleeds to death point
While they align with churches and parties

Lands they formerly appeased and guarded
They now exchange with grazers for coins
These Fons and Chiefs
Who in yesteryears were venerated
And royally greeted with cupped hands
The peoples and Fons in their insides
Have been strangled to death
By their gullibility and love for cash

They now chant hosannas and fly flags
From bamboozling churches and parties
Like headless, brainless MPs in Ngoa-Ekelle
These Fons and Chiefs
Who fonify bastard state thieves
They cry crazily
As their lands and peoples
Dessert them and serve them dishes of insolence

(Mbankolo, 7 September 2012)

Dividing Calabash

The calabash unites
It never ever disunites
That's why it is round
Like the football that unites
Players and fans and nations

But in my village
But in Mbesa
A calabash divides
Like an unbridged river
And mercilessly kills
Like a provoked python
It must have been misused

The calabash unites
It never ever disunites
That's why it is round
Like the egg that harbours
Yoke and albumen and chicks

But in my village
But in Mbesa
A calabash divides
Like an unbridged river
And mercilessly kills
Like a provoked python
It must have been misused

The calabash unites
never ever disunites
That's why it is round

Like the world that hosts
Blacks and whites and reds

But in my village
But in Mbesa
A calabash divides
Like an unbridged river
And mercilessly kills
Like a provoked python
It must have been misused

The calabash unites
It never ever disunites
That's why it is smooth
Like the cemented floor that accepts
Parents and children and visitors

But in my village
But in Mbesa
A calabash divides
Like an unbridged river
And mercilessly kills
Like a provoked python
It must have been misused

(Mbankolo, 29 March 2013)

Real Sons And Daughters

Real sons
put on black thread-caps
and Bamenda-regalias
and cow-skin sandals
and drink in horns and calabashes
from fibre-bags hanging on their shoulders.
They carry these everywhere they go
like donkeys carry the white strips
on their faces.

Real sons
go around with their cultures
like tortoises go around with their
rough backs.

Taking-cultures live as long as flies
            while
giving-cultures live as long as stones.

Real daughters
wear cowried hairdos or headscaffs
and Beti-kabbas
and sheep-skin low heels
and drink in nutshells and calabashes
from bamboo-baskets hanging on their shoulders.
They carry these everywhere they go
like girafes carry the black and white spots
on their skins.

Real daughters

move about with their cultures
like snails move about with their
segmented shells.

Imitating-cultures are run-offs
            while
imitated cultures are rivers.

(Mbankolo, 26 August, 2013)

Dry Season In Mbesa

Heaven's sorrows are no more
Since weeping Toto Mbels shed no tears.
Muddy, watery, slippery motor paths don't bore.
Swift, sporadic nimbus lights spread no fears,
But by day angry Sun murders crops
And by night deaf and dumb winds freeze all.
Like abandoned Shakespearean props
On stage, dust-coated shrubs and trees fall
To moan our miasmic cultures and values
Left to melt away into confusion and droughts
While Wonatok and Nchisadoase draw death daggers
At Mbeh's scattering whistle which manures
Domestic disorder that breeds cultural droughts
Into futures as black as skins of rock badgers.

(Monatélé II, 10 January 2013)

The Young and the Old

Chorus:
The world is an orange
And life is a car-tyre
They never change
They're constant like stones
Only Man changes
Only Man regresses

Young Man:
On Modernity's wings we fly like swallows
Reaching high technological skies
Harvesting phones, radios, and computers
Quitting our black cultural shells
Inhaling toxic white cultural smokes
And celebrating this free Freedom
Freedom for men and men
Freedom for women and women
Freedom for children and children
To freely reverse Nature and
To freely tie nuptial knots

Life is sprouting like buds
We're no less than the Old
Since rights are ours too
We're manured- and fertilized-kids
Always happy, very happy, very happy
But Aging Climate makes us cry
We regret these waterless valleys
And grassless mountains
And treeless forests
Which dispatch doom-emissaries

To announce lifeless/dreamless tomorrows
To our stone-ears, to our dead-ears

Old Man:
Everything that was
Is and shall always be
No new hills, no new stones
No new forests, no new rivers
Good days are gone
Tough days are now
Tougher days are coming
The Young gestate doom and trouble

But when we were young
Our fathers fallowed our mothers
And there were no condoms
And there was no HIV and AIDS

But when we were toddlers
Our fathers had us beaten
And we rode on right paths
And we espoused respect and reason

But when we were kids
Our fathers had many, many wives
And no woman was husbandless
And no woman went to Miniferme

Today we are old and same
While you are young and mutating
You clamour for change
And change comes in company:

In the company of numberless deaths
In the company of invincible diseases
In the company of unnatural sex deals
In the company of Climate Change

River:
Blow not the trumpets of Change
Join not the chorus of Progress
Where are my new brother-rivers?
Life is a constant tyre
Spinning on a constant divine axis

Is Change dwindling rains?
Is Change drying rivers?
Is Change withering plants
On the banks of waterless rivers?
Is Change thirsty fish learning
To swim on dusty riverbeds?

If Yes, then Change shouldn't change.

Young Fon:
Marbled mansions palace us
No more thatches, no more mud
Four-legged houses transport us
No more trekking, no more horses

Jehovah's worship calls us
No more shrines, no more rituals
One-wifed palaces for us
No more polygamy, no more polyproblems

Party politics concerns us
No more neutrality, no more poverty
The rich shake hands with us
No more dignity, no more poverty

Hardworking servants win our love
And are awarded calabashes for medals
Change is good, Change is good
But why these wranglings?

Brother tribes draw daggers over land
Princes and Nchindas hark each other
And Culture loses its lustre
And rusts like unprotected iron

Old Fon:
Listen, oh Young Fon, to this!
Good days have walked into the past
You celebrate nothing but blind Change
All new things now have traps and snares

In my days, Fons were Kings,
Greeted with cupped-hands
From a distance of respect and honour
They were special, very special

From head to toe they were special
Special in their heavy embroideries
Special in their political neutrality
Special in their religious plurality

41

Inside and outside, they were special
Special as they drank alone from horns and calabashes
Special as they spoke wisdom
Special as they had self-respect

But today, Fons are toys
They're remote-controlled beggars
Selling out dignities to servants
Scrambling to beg from politicians

They defecate on Thrones and Crowns
They exchange holy lands for coins
They breed tribal sagas and wars
And plant disunity among brothers and sisters

Deaths spread across their lands
Like wild fires on dry-season hills
While they celebrate blind Change
And extend invitations to Climate Change

Mountain:
From time immemorial I am a Mountain
Reigning as King of the Lowlands
I've never seen a new Mountain
Yet songs of Change animate the Lowlands

Life is as constant as the Northern Star
Under the skies, everything is Old
Everything that was in the beginning is now
And ever shall be, world without end

The only Change I know
Is the Sun's rudeness these days
The only Change I know
Are frequent fires on me these days

The only Change I see
Is the retiring and tiring rainfall
The only Change I see
Are rivers growing pale like AIDS' patients

Young Woman:
We were air in yesteryears
Men crushed our rights and lives
Like vehicles crushing road-ants
When on mad speeds on our death-tracks
Like a broom gathering dirt
A man would gather us as wives
And install us for delivery machines
Fuelled with fertile liquids from his pipe

Our rights and mights are ours now
Who marries us is our choice
'One man, one wife' is the rule
Colour and race walls have all collapsed
'One wife, one wife' is not bad
When we like, no liquid from them
Ever reaches our fertile soils
Except stubborn rains from HIV/AIDS
Which join Aging Climate to murder us
Before we reach Mother Sarah's age

Old Woman:
We bowed to greet our Husbands
In the good old days of life
When one mighty Man would call
Many of us into a happy and peaceful union
We would dress like our mothers
In animal-skins, cowries and necklaces
And shake our bodies to ancestral beats
Without raping our Husbands in public

Today the world is upside-down
The Young have broken the bone of secrets
In search of the marrow of Wisdom
And for their stubbornness and impatience
They have been served madness and death
In the madness women marry women
And mad men marry mad men
And bring forth incurable diseases
Which combine forces with Aging Climate
To bring life to a premature end

Tree:
No new trees have been seen
No new Heaven and Earth have been
Nothing new has been created
Where then is the Change you chant?

The only Change is Climate Change
Innocent trees murdered without successors
Green bushes reduced to ashes and smoke
Wandering smokes violate Ozone's privacy
Homeless animals stray into human traps

Angry pregnant rivers destroy homes and lives
Elsewhere rain's gates are locked
So that everything grows from worse to worst

Chorus:
The world is an orange
And life is a car-tyre
They never change
They're constant like stones
Only Man changes
Only Man regresses

(Between Mbankolo and Monatélé II, between 8 April and 16 May, 2013)

Black Redeemer

(*For Nelson Mandela*)

He has borne our troubles,
The white crimes on black skins.

He fought fiercely, yet harmlessly,
Creating Umkhonto for you and me.

Long, long road to Calvary he took,
Completing twenty seven Stations of the Cross,

Weeping to see barrels of black blood
Flowing past him down like Niles

While the Human watersheds
Feed billions of maggots and vultures.

Barred doors were the nails
That crucified him at Polls Moore.

Like Jesus, he preaches peace today
While Nosekeni and Mary radiate in Heaven

(Mbankolo, 22 December 2012)

The Name Ngam

(For Christopher Ngam Nsom & Emmanuel Beyia Ngam)

Some names die
Before their bearers and disappear
Like ghosts leaving no traces
Some names curse
And frustrate their bearers and ruin them
By erasing further survival chances
Some names like
Daffodils blossom at dawn in goodness
And wither at dusk in evil along their bearers

But a name
I know which outlives bearers
And spreads her warm wings
On many like Sun's rays
On Earth

Yes, a name
I have known which rubs afflicted hearts like balm
And overflows hers banks in kindness and humility

A generous name
I know which like a Mother Hen gathering her chickens
Gathers orphans and wipes their tears

Ngam is the name

In GSS Mbessa
Ngam (Emmanuel Beyia) fathers and tutors me
sweet sweet French/Literature lessons

My first play
He proofreads and urges me
To write and write and write and write and write
In humility

In CCAST Bambili
Ngam (Christopher Nsom) fathers, tutors and mentors me
In sweet sweet Literature lectures
My drama anthology's blurb
He writes and urges me
To write and study and study and write and write and study
In generosity

The name Ngam
Has lighted flames
Of creativity in my heart
And continues to fan these flames
Making me mount
The stairs of challenge
With hope and confidence

(Mbankolo, 21 September 2012)

Special Brother
(For Ngong Emmanuel Nsani)

Never given to anger he's knowN
Going miles molding minds of younG
Orderliness and love he clings tO
Negotiating progress too for the unborN
Giving generously; yet hardly ever takinG

Eager to love with a heart purE
Managing mistakes to levels minimuM
Maintaining flow of kindness like a streaM
Actively present in times of need and fiestA
Neat in dressing like a queeN
Undoes stubbornness like a ZulU
Ever willing to instill in us lovE
Love towards all: the short and talL

Nothing can for long make him frowN
Since he finds no pleasure in sorrowS
And knows happiness is sweet like FantA
None like him I've ever before seeN
Indeed rare and special like a champion skI

(Mbankolo, 30 December 2012)

Caring Carine

(For Carine Kes NGONG)

As a mother hen is caring,
So too you are caring, very caring.

As summer rain is generous,
So too you are generous, very generous.

As a red, road-crossing ant is hard-working,
So too you are hardworking, very hardworking.

I grovel at your feet
To salute your open-handedness,
To appreciate your humility,
To congratulate your perseverance,
To preach your uniqueness.

Your soft voice magnetizes us
To your company, making us
Crumble in heaps below your
Tall, beautiful, and cheerful form
And thank Feyiyn for His endless wonders,
For His endless wonders of creation,
The wonders of creating you.

(Mbankolo, 29 March 2013)

Without Shallote

In Your Absence,
I drowsily drag myself
like a millipede along the dry banks
of the valleys of loneliness.

These valleys are all dull and dry,
so dry, so dry, so dry, so dry
and empty like a vacuum
because you are absent.

I write Shallotte
on sandy dunes
and wild winds blow it off,
leaving no traces behind.

Then I remember a place
where I engraved that name
the very first day I saw you
and wind cannot access it:

The place is hidden behind
my chest; it is my heart
and Shallotte is engraved
there in indelible, golden letters.

(Monatéle II, January 18, 2013)

Success Time Is Here

(For Shallotte Jenkuo)

Even
as failure
roars across
the nation from
GCE Board in Buea 2012,
you've made it…You've engraved
your golden Onion name—Shallotte—among
the selected few: the laborious ones, the hardworking ones,
the meritorious ones. Here is Success smiling at you, skipping
from side to side,
 beckoning you to sky-limit heights. Snore not on your
laureates; rise up and up and up.

High
School is rushing
home, whistling melodies
of perseverance for you. Drinks and cakes
behind you; long winding paths of thorns and toils lure you
hopefully into the future. In this gloomy, smoky land, you
must toil upwards.

My
heart's laden
with profound joy, the joy
of your success, our success. Never
worry! Firmly grip your plume in your ever-
 snowy fingers and scribble…think and write, write and think.

I can
feel the bliss
of your joy blowing across
your Dad's homestead, planting ecstasies
of celebration, gathering friends and relatives in unison.
 In the sweet, sweet melodies of festivities, I chant the songs
of love.
I crisscross my legs in the perpetual dance of incessant love,
thanking the
Most High for the gift of your romantico-Kennethic heart.
Bravoooooooooooooo!

Six
papers are not
a joke. They incarnate long
 lonely nights of studies and nine long
months of shuttling between GBPHS Yaounde and
 Mbankolo. A countless number of times have your feet
frantically ascended and descended Milingui's Hill. Frequent
light cuts
locked you up in dark ,dark rooms, winding and rewinding
your brains.

In
these six
triangular stanzas
of verses, the flag of your pyrrhic
victory is hoisted. I am the flagstaff and
you are the nylon rope transporting your achievements
up and down the staff. Dying out in the distance are the
ices

from your Dad's sitting room that distracted you, echoing disorderly across
your cerebral membranes, pumping dreadful blood through your veins and seriously
warning you against failure. Finally, success is here! Behold dawn lights of more success!

(Mbankolo, Thursday 2 August, 2012;
GCE results having been released on Monday 31 July 2012)

Toiling Widow

(For my mother Nawain Prisca Ansama)

Victim of nightmarish polygamy
        Though Second
Loved and cherished by husband
        Skunk of
The world when husband freezes

Legion heirs pour in
Born of vacuums far off
From husband's pedigree and cow
You and your eight sons
Down to misery and hardships

Where are your marital sisters?
        Husband's First
Third and Fourth Sweeties
        Posthumous sagas
Have scattered and flung them apart

Their greed and egoism
Drove you away from
Your mediocre mansion
Into your kids' shanties
Where the wretched should live

You've taught me that
        Polygamy is
A cactus fence of love wherein
        The powerful
Jealous prey on the weak innocents

Your Darling's premature departure
Wiped away all smiles on
Your face and turned you
Into a suffering object that
Lives on forehead sweat and tears

From dawn to dusk
          Your hoe
Digs in and out of Earth
          Like beetles
For your Benjamin's success' seek

Throttle not to a halt Mom
Keep your heart idling
Like a lorry's engine
Till I fuel you with joy
Since I am your only Benjamin

(Carrière, 29 August 2012)

For Prisca Ansama

(In honour of my Mom)

Hardly does the world
Notice saints like you
When they're still alive,
But when you become shadows,
Your praises flood us,
Overflowing world banks
Into familial valleys
Where neglect and jealousy began.

From Nsah's beloved wife
To a rejected suffering widow,
Jilted out of corrugated iron roofs
To collect rains under sons'
Leaking grass huts
And to snuggle down to futons
Each time God's falling tears
Clatter and splash outside at night.

Your willing palms have gripped
Indefatigable hoes for years,
Searching through Earth like
Chinese bulldozers or pigs
To gather the gold and silver
That has kept me steadily
Upwards on academic ladders
And on slippery stairs of challenge.

Exemplary Mom, waves of advice
Connect your mouth to my ears:

'Kenneth, a suffering orphan has no father.
All men you see should be your fathers.
Respect all women as if they're me,
For a poor person's child must respect.'
This plus your love plus your prayers
Are catapulting me into genuine success.

The ominous news of your frequent coughs,
Fevers and wounded legs strikes
My spinal cord like electric current.
I tremble and tremble and shiver
Like an epicenter for fear of unknowns.
I fear Angels want to dine with you,
But budge not Sweet Mom till
You savour the joys of your labour.

(Mbankolo, 29 August 2012)

The Joy Of Studies

My heart sings sweet, sweet songs
when I am in class,
grasping new meanings,
balancing new and complicated equations
like a mathematical magician.

When I am in Second Monatélé
weighing down on benches,
in readiness to memorize new words
in English and French,
then my soul says it's sufficient
because it responds to drums
of bilingualism from across Cameroon.

I stop foolishly watching the télé
when I hear school bells ringing
and calling you and me to school;
through dusty paths I rush
fearing not the sand-carrying lorries
because I know that my tomorrow
is very, very bright if I study hard today.

There is joy in studies.
There is real joy in serious studies,
where there is real discipline and respect,
where students don't run away from English,
where students don't drink King Arthur,

59

where students don't come late to school.

(Monatélé II, January 24, 2013)

Make Sounds For Pounds

Who thinks opportunities are few
and joins the unending queue
to scramble like cats for mice,
erasing chances as much as rice?

Chances abound for those who dare
and take good risks with much care
here below these starry skies
where we must fend like flies.

When all seems to fail,
follow your vocal trail;
clear your throat and make the sounds
that will bring you the needed pounds.

You turn around and find nothing,
come round and create something.
And like Shakespeare write the books
that will become your success hooks.

You fear failure in every room?
Summon your courage like a groom
and search these rooms for the bride
who will contribute to your pride.

After school no work?
Work hard and keep wake.
Use the skills in your brain
to get money from those you train.

Stop complaining like a fool.
Go to a good sports school
and train your hands or legs
to become your success pegs.

Nothing for you to eat?
Leave that soft seat,
and sweat to sow the vegetables
that will freshen your tables.

(Monatélé II, 14 March 2013)

When the poet nauseates as decency, morality and dignity are slaughtered...

Musical Madness

On pornographic podiums of dance
Are heard heavy satanic hissings
            And crazy choirs
Solidly surrounded with twitters
Vomiting madly maddening Freedom
            And Human Rights
Mocking Feyiyn, mocking morality
Mocking Africa, mocking morality
            And disgracing decency

With dancers dressed half naked
We see chest-melons rise and fall
            While dancers vibrate
Like erupting, angry Mount Fako
And sway heads left and right
            Like mad lizards
Male onlookers wet inner wears
In extreme excitement while
            Bikutsi and Makossa
Lure feeble fellows and fools
Into new Sodoms and Gomorrahs
            Beastifying Mankind forever

(Mbankolo, 30 and 31 December 2012)

Righting Feyiyn's Wrongs

The natural, nice brows
Have lost their hair
To the deforesting hands
Of beauty surgeons and satans
The beautiful black hair
Are now powdery brown & black

These women are righting Feyiyn's wrongs
And multiplying His wrath by more wrongs

See nude breasts on chests
Hanging like Eden's tempting fruits
No longer twin top-taps for babies
Exposed like wares on sale
These soft, pointed chest melons
Invite you and me to serious sex sins

These women are righting Feyiyn's wrongs
And multiplying His wrath by more wrongs

Sexy skirts far, far above knees
Permanently folding upwards towards
The hidden house of procreation and pleasure
White palms with very long fingers
And red, red nails keep coming
Down to pull the stubborn skirts downwards

These women are righting Feyiyn's wrongs
And multiplying His wrath by more wrongs

This black beauty is unbalanced
On these five-metre high heels
Trekking in towns and villages
Distributing immune deadly diseases
Yet moving at snail speed
To avoid the shame of falling

These women are righting Feyiyn's wrongs
And multiplying His wrath by more wrongs

Feyiyn was blind to beautify brows with hair
Feyiyn was brainless to make breasts for babies
Feyiyn was dull to dress Eve below knees
Feyiyn was foolish to make feet flat
Woman is right to shave brows and advertise breasts
Woman is right to be nude on very high heels

These women are righting Feyiyn's wrongs
And multiplying His wrath by more wrongs

(Mbankolo, 31 December 2012)

Beasts' Response

*(This is an imaginative response of Beasts
to "Beats on Two Legs", a poem published in Chaining Freedom,
2012)*

When humans go crazy
And lick their exit holes
In the name of freedom
And force sex pistons
Through ovals meant
For metabolic waste
You cannot rub that on us
You cannot link that to us
You cannot blame that on us
You cannot justify that in us

When man and man
Woman and woman
Rub bodies together
In ecstasies of craziness
Like two mad dogs
In a sex match
And call that Human Rights
You cannot term them beasts
You cannot find fault in beasts
You cannot bury your miasmas in beasts
You cannot empty your dark bowels into beats

When a father
Caresses a daughter
And serves her from
Her mother's love vessels

In order to engulf more wealth
Like an amoeba does with food
That is not beastly but satanic
That is not beastly but hellish
That is not beastly but demonic
That is not beastly but devilish

When brother and sister
Eat groin fruits and stick mouths
Together under innocent blankets
And blood-stain white wool
With dark red incestuous liquids
And assassinate Holy Writings for pleasure's seek
Humans should not look to beasts
Humans should rather copy from beasts
Humans should learn from beasts
Humans should emulate beasts

When in Syria men slash men's throats
While in Mali humans are ground like maize
By humans for maggot consumption
While in Nigeria Musa and John draw daggers
Like David and Goliath over One God
Who has a panoply of names and yet is One
There is danger in the Human Kingdom
There is trouble and there'll be floods this Kingdom
There is fire on the Mountain of Freedom
There is an error on the Human page and kingdom

And the time to act is slipping
Out of Human palms now and here
And meandering, leaving no dust

Into the limbos of existence
While Humans wallow in moral misery
Scanning the air for where and whom to blame
And they can only see and blame beasts
And they can only sit and accuse beasts
And they can only idle by to point beasts
And they can only in vain stain beasts

(Bastos, 13 November 2012)

When the poets laments social decay, reckless accidents and deaths...

Babies' Dump
(Following abandonment of a baby in Domayo, Northern Cameroon)

This very chilly dewy morning
when
birds
in their usual dawn obituary hymns
woke
us
up from deep, deep slumber
this
baby's
persistent cry summoned us here
to
this
cursed river side of atrocities.

This river's journeying waters
have
been
witnesses to the sinistre act
of
this
very unlucky chilly morning—they
observed
this
innocent baby born and abandoned here
by

her
own loving and caring mother.

Like Bethlehem's manger this
swollen
refuse
heap was the delivery room
where
this
unclothed crying baby came forth
into
this
thorny planet of heartless humans
to
find
himself wrapped up in his bloody umbilical cord.

See blood here and see blood there
which
oozed
out like a river from the wicked Mom
of
this
premature but healthy baby we
are
now
transporting to Maroua Central Hospital
to
number
the eighth baby abandoned in ten months.

(Mbankolo, Thursday 23 August 2012)

Head In A Bag

(Following an incident in which a 25-year-old
boy cut his father's head in Buea, in March 2013)

He was my father
And I was his son
But I had to become rich
But I had to become rich
Very rich, very rich, very rich
As rich as Michelle Fotso
Then he would be as rich
As Victor Fotso in his tomb

My father's head
 In
My big, big bag
 For
My much money

I waylaid my father
In the farm like a real son
My well-filed machete
Came down on his old neck
Like a Guillotine
Then blood oozed
Then blood oozed
And blood gargled
And blood gargled
To stain my innocent face
And bless me into affluence

71

My father's head
 In
My big, big bag
 For
My much money

I washed my father's head
In the farm like a real son
Wrapped the head in
Black, black plastic papers
In readiness to export
For my much money
Just to be caught unawares
Like a kid defecating in the backyard.

My father's head
 In
My big, big bag
 For
My much money

(Mbankolo, 27 March 2013)

Mimboman

Cold winds fluff
Through dumb tree branches
While wide horizons
Blink Eastern pupils, heralding dawn

The dull sky overlooks
This villainous earth
And even birds cannot sing
And even crickets cannot croak

There is shame and terror
There is terror and shame
In the Mimboman open-air mortuary
Outskirting treacherous Yaoundé

Here is a human corpse
Charming clouds of flies
With nauseating odours
And weeping human flesh

Colonies of happy flies
Occasionally scatter into the air
While fat, whitish maggots
Dig in and out of the rotting meat

Here is both mortuary and grave
Yawning wounds conspicuously
Sit where breasts and genitals
Stood when this victim was alive

Who committed this holy atrocity?
Where are the mutilated parts?
Was this victim male or female?
Who uses human parts and why?

Perhaps, some drugged riff-raffs
Drugged him or her in darkness
To get fresh flesh for some rites
To propel some white-coated boss into power

(Mbankolo, 08 April 2013)

Tonga 2011

*(In Memory of all those who perished in the high way accident
that occurred at Tonga in 2011)*

The year 2011
Goes on retirement
In a mournful convoy
In Tongaland
Where crazy flames of fire
Have devoured more than 30

Through one man's
Unreasoned action
Like that of Adam
Many are condemned
To perish in flames on Earth
And to rejuvenate in souls in Heaven

What could be
The colour of souls
From burned bodies?
Who is to blame
For this undesired roasted human meat?
Reckless conductor
Who parked petrol tanker
Along a footpath highway
Or
Snoozing Amour Mezam Chauffeur
Who ran into
Carelessly-parked tanker
On serpentine footpath highway
Or

Meandering stretches of
Potholes that connect
Minor quantity of Kamerun
In the name of Highways?

When my ink waters papers
With stinging tears of Tonga
Emissaries of CRTV bad news
Invade my heart like angry bees
And announce tantalizing news
Of 18 deaths and 35 injuries
Recorded in two days only
On Bafoussam's roads only

Obvious it becomes
That forever our roads
Shall bear names
Such as Death Triangle
And be deadly decorated
With warning sign posts
Shouting and whispering
X or Y deaths here
Even in our blind march
Towards eclipsing
Emergence in 2035

(Mbankolo, 17 and 21 September 2012)

Mournful Mondays

Christ defeated Death on Sunday
But Death strikes on Monday
Invisible forces Monday have chosen
To have little angels frozen
With tumbling waters in unison

May fourteen 2012 was a Monday
Murderous droplets and blood-thirsty clay
Crushed three little Foys in Mbankolo
Monday third June 2013 above Mokolo
Furious run-off drowned two daughters low

In Mbankolo, crowds stream
To see helpless parents scream
Over three little coffins like in a dream
In Carrière, countless humans flow
In to mourn two daughters as tears flow

(Mbankolo, 12 June 2013)

Syrian And Other Graveyards

Unnumbered human corpses
mutilated and spread
like illegally-shot elephants in Waza Park!
From 'man know thyself'
to 'man hates himself'-
humans mutilate humans!

Future-bound glorious infants,
feeble moms and luck-abandoned dads
bombed, suffocated, shot and slain
by politico-economic drunks!
Yawning stomachs here,
blood-dripping arms there,
open-mouth frozen heads here,
rotting breasts there,
decomposing legs here…

We are in Homs,
we are in Alep,
we are in Damascus where
 there has been fierce fighting
since long ago…

Vultures in black suits
brace up for carnivorous autopsy;
they transport chunks from
the uninterred corpses to
carnivorous mortuaries up-sky.
Maggots, ants and scavengers
perform rapid interments,

substituting caskets and graves
with their innards and
facilitating the cycle from dust to dust.

These mean creatures,
some flying,
others crawling
and some others walking,
feast on the garbage corpses,
mocking man's inhumanity to man
and celebrating
this sudden twist of values—
the beastification of humans and
the humanisation of beasts.

They mock us,
they mock us
for this sudden twist of values.
They also mock us and bemoan
the occidental-egoistic planes
that burned
infinite barrels
of exploitation fuel on Libyan skies,
urinating bombs and missiles,
grinding and crushing humans for humans
or humans for oil.

Aha! What a twist of values!
Exploitation went mad
and naked in Bengazi…

We are in Homs,
we are Alep,
we are in Damascus
where all Pauls
have gone Sauls…

Annan can't understand
Libyan
 humanitarians' whereabouts
now. His six points
repose in occidental dust bins.
Then he sighs.
Then he sighs,
 performs Pilatism
and gives up.

Moscow and London persistently draw parallels
that can only meet magically in Damascus.
So-called World Powers now ride snails to
Syrian emergency meetings
while they were flown in swallows to Tripoli.

We are in Homs,
we are in Alep,
we are in Damascus
where countless infinities
of Arab eyes have focused
on one cushion since last years:
one cushion of thorns and pleasure,
one cushion of spikes and leisure…

In Bangui, Bozize's political epilepsy
Has created endless cemeteries
As endpoints for meandering blood rivers.

Blunt and filed machetes, guns and bombs
Crisscross brotherly camps boiling with religious madness
Spreading countless, mutilated human corpses
And scratching off innocent grass from earth
And pushing up temperature readings
On eco-pol thermometers.

See gold- and diamond-thirsty cousins from afar
With broad smiles busy stopping bombs and guns they sell,
And scratching the earth to locate new mines
For vertical win-win deals when the foreign rain ceases.

See corpses on exhibition in Northern Naija!
Careful, lest flooding human blood drown you!
See helpless girls imprisoned within unnamed prisons
Since long ago; see black veils on innocent, beautiful heads;
See wailing moms and dads sucked pale by stress, sun and
rain
Since abduction and adoption day long ago!

Boko is haram, but boko-produced guns and bombs are not!
Boko is haram, but boko-driven technology is a means!
Boko is haram, but boko-trained sponsors are friends!
More blood flows, more meat is served maggots and vultures
While boko-medico wizards battle with Ebola in white
aprons…

This is Ukraine. This is Ukraine. This is Ukraine
Where language opiates brothers and sisters
Distant uncles and aunts selling packaged ideas
Sow disorder within them; disorder that kills like Ebola.
Count not these corpses littered here and there!
Measure not these human liquids flooding here and there!
Watch your transport bird, lest wandering riffles and missiles
Bring you down to swell the corpse numbers and blood
volumes…

(Mbankolo, 6 August 2012; also retouched to include Bangui,
Naija and Ukraine, while in Istanbul, 26 Nov. 2014)

When the poet decries the desecration of hygiene/sanitation and environment…

Dirt and Rubbish

My waxed ears can hear
The silent piercing cries
Of the Throne which tries
In vain to voice its mute fear

Given that King B has clocked
A third ten while his accomplices
Grind teeth, peeping through keyholes of vices
Behind the bars where they're flogged

For their futile efforts to uproot
The Palace Baobab in these slums
Of politics—in these bins and slums
Where Anglo-Franco craziness nurtures its root

In these three decades of confusion
Like pigs we have dug in and out of political mud
Looking for gold but always finding rust, dust and mud
While wandering empty bottles cause pollution

And diseases in our towns and cities
The King's men & slaves swim like fish
In black, black affluence & luxuries on the Beach
Of Corruption—theirs are eternal foggy niceties

When but King B bleats like a he-goat
 His slavish thieves and supporters
Sail into orgies of deceitful applauses & like supporters
Of an ever-winning soccer team they cling to his coat

They cluster up behind his dark coats
And devour national cakes unseen
And misdirect wandering state coins unseen
Into their yawning & hungry vaults & pockets of coats

Within these decades of lurking terror
Royal Limousines have always swept across
The Airport-Palace serpentine track to cross
And re-cross the Atlantic and bomb terror

Crusaders in alien lands and implant peace
Out there His Highness shares smiles
Creating reservoirs to hide our village files
While sounding trumpets of the gun-point peace

His wild dogs instill here—countless heads
Have rolled while barrels of our blood
Like petrol rushing out of SONARA's flood
Have gushed out of us to save our heads

(Bastos, 9, 12 and 13 November 2012)

Garbage Song

Here's a solace farm
for the wretched of our land
but here's a waste basket
for the greedy rich…

Half-nude men and women
flip flap and flip flap
here in my stomach in
response to the errands
of their noisy stomachs.
Mad men and lunatic women
rush here for food and shelter
while ingrates come with urine
to pour sand into poor's *garri*.

Here's a solace farm
for the wretched of our land
but here's a waste basket
for the greedy rich…

Kids pull in sacks of bread
from the tables of the rich
and dump here at dawn and
at noon and at dusk and at night
who cares about hungry neighbours?
vehicles drive in unopened milk tins
cooked and uncooked meat to
leave here for their maggot friends
and carry their lords to Church.

Here's a solace farm
for the wretched of our land
but here's a waste basket
for the greedy rich…

Half bottles of gin
Clatter against bones
all brought in from mansions
as crumbs from greedy homes
where Bible copies abound
and contain no Lazarus
but only the Rich Man.
The poverty gap and bridge
Begin and end here.

Here's a solace farm
for the wretched of our land
but here's a waste basket
for the greedy rich…

(Mbankolo, 31 August 2012)

The Bank Of Secrets

It's so sad and bad
That I'm a rubbish dump
In World's Dirtiest Country
I'm clad in shame and disgrace
Being an HYSACAM Dump
Wherever in Kamerun

I'm mostly hungry
While offices and roads
Classrooms and churches
Bedrooms and living rooms
Verandas and gutters
Are constipated with my food

It's so sad and sorrowful
That I'm a bank of secrets
For the few who come
To feed and fill me
Like the seas and oceans
I conceal their heathen deeds

The lifeless baby in me
Was brought in this morning
By her righteous Mom
Before skies opened their eyes
She ran into church
And walked out into Miniferme

Laden with human bones
My intestines were last week

Following the grandiose feast
Tycoons organized down town
To celebrate Mr X's First Billion
And accost new aspirants

This water down my cheeks
Is urine very dangerous urine
From a young drunken graduate
Who's distributed barrels of HIV
To tens of teenagers in
Exchange for examination marks

Some humans empty bowels
Into me under night's wings
After long tiring days of work
In toiletless offices and homes
Hygiene and morals are dead
They only care about life

Blood drinkers steal in
After sun's sleep to drop
Luxurious waste and
Ensnare and trap the poor
Who call me Mom and cook
And honour rendezvous like clock birds

My environs are brothels
Young singles connect here
Unfaithfuls steal fruits here
They all load me with waste
Adulterous condoms and …
Their secrets' store is here

(Between Mbankolo and Carrière,
29 and 31 August 2012)

Hygienic Corruption

What is Corruption?
Anything substituting merit
Commercialization of consciences
Coins and groins
Bustling up and down
To thwart plans
In High Bureaus and
Magically uprooting meritorious
Names on exam/job lists…

State ministers and governors
Like lice and ticks
Feed on their host coffers
And like mad dogs
Swindle the sums
They should guard and protect
Contracts advertised in
Family Meetings
And roads tarred on paper…

My pens soak papers
With inky tears
As I bemoan this new birth
The birth of Hygienic Corruption
Empty rubbish dumps and
Half-filled garbage cans
Mock our loss of values
While dirt floods and floats
In houses and offices and streets and…

(Mbankolo, 3 August 2012)

Hovering Above Yaoundé

1.
Rusty serpentine roads
meander through yawning
heaps of frightening garbage
depicting
a people of lost values,
a people of dead hygiene.

Cholera's sirens
echo and re-echo across
the protruding
walls of cherished garbage
and stagnant germ pounds,
healing filth-ridden residents
and whispering benedictions
of nausea.

2.
Immaculately-clothed damsels and lasses,
hands pregnant with food,
board yellow mobile houses
for restaurants. When windows
squat, flying peelings, tincans,
biscuit sacks…collapse
onto muddy-dusty-tarred paths,
some repairing infinite potholes,
others heightening mountains of refuse.

3.

In praise-singing houses,
juicy ministers before
pale and sickly followers
tell tales of unseen pleasures
and treasures, caring no damn
about souls and hygiene.
Priestly financiers cajole
desperate salvation slaves
into flooding sanctuaries
with gifts and cash
while
littering God's House with
angry muddy lettuces
and smiling floating plastic bags.
Out of bounds
to greediness
and hygiene!
Cleanliness is next to Satanliness!

Cholera and malaria,
arm-in-arm, walk in
in concertation, in response
to our numerous invitations.
Wrapped in black *ngandouras*,
they begin the haphazard
selection of students for hygiene
lessons in theatres and mortuaries.

4.

In lecture rooms, sparkly
tutors care no damn about

health and hygiene as they
under- and over-dose learners
with worthless knowledge—
impracticable definitions and
improvable calculations.
Impeccable classrooms,
carpeted with pebbles,
rotting peelings,
decomposing cockroaches,
chattering plastic bags
and immortal tincans.
Under desks and
under lockers,
we hear dirt snoring,
chattering, stealing lessons,
diffusing undesired perfumes
and multiplying hospital bills.
Half-nude damsels
with reddened lips and
hyper-bleached visages
in the company of lazy crazy
westernized boys make nuptial
plans in electronic madness.

5.
In commercial centres,
decaying foodstuff,
dung beetles, scavengers,
ants, maggots, hairless gaunt dogs,
dying tomatoes and
mangoes queue up
to pay homage

to ignorant traders.
They mingle with
Buyer-awaiting products,
conceiving and concealing
imminent sporadic
outbreaks of deadly maladies…
In these rubbish dump markets,
diseases are commercialized
behind the filthy money
and venomous merchandise
that migrate
between buyers and sellers.

Cholera and his likes
tiptoe in and out
in readiness
to pounce on their prey
when they
must
have
murdered hygiene right
into their homes and mouths.

6.
Situations turn sourer
at home.
Humans and dirt are
bedfellows; bugs and
caterpillars are witnesses
to all acts on
matrimonial beds.
Banana and cane peelings

are tiles;
plastic bags and rags
are carpets
while tincans and used-lotion bottles
are alarm clocks.
Dirtiness is acquired
alongside mother tongues
since dust bins and garbage cans
are too expensive to procure
and HYZACAM is never near enough...
Charity ends at home?

(Mbankolo, 10 August 2012)

Mokolo Slums

1.
In these centrally-located
far ends of Yaoundé
we dwell—
Mokolo Elobi.

We are the Cinderellas
of the Beti Regime
which has exiled us
to this desert of hope
since we are too dark for life
and are kinsmen of Babatoura
our First Kaiser.

We are the cipher
of the Yaoundé clique
piled up in
these healthy swampy slums
where potable sources
and pit latrines
and rubbish dumps
are connected like computers
in a cybercafé
into our stomach servers.

While our brother potters
chatter and clatter
stolen pots
filling the air with unfriendly noises
which reverberate like

the claptrap of His Excellency's
electoral campaigns,
our lumped children
roam around stinging garbage
and cluttering verandas with
smiling excrement
which beckon on Cholera
to dine with us.

2.

When Cholera finally invades
these conspicuous slums,
our human herds dwindle
into limbos,
but when these epidemic tides
calm down,
idleness transforms us
into snuggling and snogging
machines
which swell the slums
with innocent
futureless bastards.

3.

When the Sun goes to sleep,
terrible exodus occurs here:
countless winos clad in black
cockroach-eaten, sweat-urine-scenting rags,
murderous bandits in black masks
and nubile young girls in black mini-skirts
follow circuitous paths
and disappear

into the heart of town—
the very heart of evil.

While we feed on chunder
in these slums,
His Excellency's crumbs
flood HYSACAM dumps
and we must only chunter
about our glorious plight
for fear
of his numberless drogued soldier ants.

(Mbankolo, 20 August 2012)

When the poet bemoans Man's distortion of the ecological balance...

Dry Season

The dropping drums on housetops
Have ceased this season.

The sky frowns no more.
From dawn to dusk it now smiles.

The angry angel spitting flames stops
Because the Sun has brought reason.

Heaven's intestines grumble no more.
Only cold, cold blisses animate nights.

New season and new troubles:
Cheap powder, leaking noses, dying plants.

Freezing lonely nights scare lovers
And we beckon the old season back.

(Mbankolo, 22 December 2012)

Environmental Foes

Dogs bark and laugh
wagging tails when
sun yawns on us
and trees jubilate
in triumphant songs
when rain comes in
in nimbus convoys

From tree and house tops
liquid drops tumble down
and man's warned/advised
to multiply woody friends
launch wars against smoke
train troops in valleys
of life's precious liquid

Send diplomats to Ozone
let birds flap wings to Ozone
and pledge our support
in invading environmental foes
battlefields are mental
since diehards despise
ringing precautions

Butterflies march across
leaf-carpeted lawns
stealing and borrowing nectar
from flowers like kids do
from meat pots when Mom
visits slumber lands

unprepared and unconscious

These marvels of April
unravel nature's treasures
for you and for me and for us
excited horses and cows
parade in herds to graze
on these lawns but without
planting chaos like you and me

At daggers drawn we are
nature's foes mingle and dine
with us like Judas while
they ready to kidnap trees
and assassinate fauna and
betray themselves ignorantly
who are enemies of Environment?

(Mbankolo, 31 August 2012)

Innocent Ozone

Celestial drops our faces do splash
While Heaven's bulbs on us do flash
Feverish fingers go up our faces
At chameleons' speed to scrub our faces
And swallow these cold angry drops
Meant for our pale crops
Which but on our faces land
To warn our races for the sand
We sprinkle across the earth's surface
Through the black toxic smokes that race
Into Innocent Ozone sowing peril
And dragging us to cliffs of more peril
As black clouds of mortal despair
Conceal the faces that toil to repair

(Bastos, 13 November 2012)

Shrubs' Emergency

Long leafy blades softly swing
From side to side on their way
Ant yet they move not, they only swing
Themselves in the wind's way.
Their parent shrubs have a meeting
With these lanky trees crying
In Man's fangs and engine saws bleeding
Them to death caring less about Ozone's crying.

This shrub assembly is urgent, very urgent.
Here Man's fate is at stake—it's an emergency.
See bird colonies flowing into this urgent
Meeting, some white, some black, to this emergency
That centres on Man. Lizards and snakes hiss
Along barren lands to talk Man's health
While Woman and Woman kiss
In their blind search for misleading wealth.

When nature's children cloister up
In the presence of dwindling rains
They cannot but look up and up
And pray Man gets out of pains.
But who makes trees pale and sickly?
Who chases away rains and rivers?
Why are plants retiring so quickly?
Where are they hasting to these flowers?
After aeons of reflection these animals
And these trees and these shrubs and insects
Have unanimously blamed special mammals
Because everything amiss Man injects

Carelessly into the environment like fools
Mixing poison into their food
And yet Men and Women have souls
While plants and animals sweat under their load.

(Bastos, Wednesday 05 December 2012)

Filtered Rays

It's a sunny morning in December
The infant sun's rays are hot like an ember

The unveiled oriental rays are indeed blinding
My eyes scan skies knowing not what they're finding

To a tree territory my friendly feet move
These few tree survivors my eyes from dangers remove

The naked sun's sons slant through leafy branches
And lose their cruel nakedness to these brotherly branches

These bridal rays now cast my shadow
Onto the green lawns opposite the window

Like bride and groom my eyes and rays maintain
While my rejoicing shadow and grass remain

On my knees I go down to confess
Man's cruelty to trees and grass: guarantors of success.

(Bastos, 06 December 2012)

Leaves On Leave

Sometimes trees' green fingers
Stand still like reposing harbingers
Of hope and despair; they meditate
On our ignorance of them who medicate
Us when diseases burgle into our souls
Taking us unawares like April fools.

At times tree branches and leaves
Come to a halt and fold up their sleeves.
Like parentless kids, they stand still,
Holding Ozone Crisis Meetings until
God's silent servants come and sway
Them from angle to angle, wiping away

The spells of fear that cloud our faces
Each time leaves go on leave leaving no traces
Of further existence for Man who digs
His graves whenever he murders figs—
The figs that link us to the Unseen Being
Who reveals His presence in Man's wellbeing.

But when God's blowing sons and daughters
Sweep across Earth, letting twigs leave their fathers,
Falling twigs and dried leaves clatter
And produce celestial music to flatter
Man while lizards play basses with tails
And flying fowls chant solos and tales.

Then Man joins this universal worship,
 Going down on knees to supplicate God's fellowship,

Feeding his doubting heart with conviction
As Christ's promises come to completion
Revealing the active hands of a Father Invisible
Who marvels His creatures with things invincible.

When these invisible but active servants of God gather
More momentum in synergy with Sun, leaves wither,
'Tree trunks go epileptic while roofs migrate
And mortal Man gets to concentrate
On these leaves and stems which go on retirement
To remind him of his own imminent retirement.

(Between Carrier and Mbankolo, Sunday 02 December 2012)

When the poet fires ink and papers against mosquitoes and disease sources...

Blood Banks

White-aproned surgeons
Inject us to heal
Like hot, hot balm
Soothes painful wounds, but
These black-skinned tiny-legged
Nocturnal surgeons
Inject us to take and to hurt.
They drain the red, red
Petrol in us for their multiplication,
Replacing it with
Their saliva of headaches and madness.

In hospital blood banks
Blood's as scarce as oases in Sahara
Because we are steadily stingy.
But when night draws nigh
And we turn to imitate death
Anopheles come imitating surgeons
Where treated nets have gone a-fishing.
These uninvited bedfellows
Come collecting red, red blood
Into dark, dark skin banks
Where no human can come a-borrowing.

Unfaithful flies!
While male mosquitoes
Wallow in wondrous loneliness

At night,
Their females dessert conjugal beds
To commit adultery
With death-mimicking human couples,
Piercing through bodies with stylets
To steal food and multiply eggs,
Luring with vhh-vhh-vhh-vhh music,
Caressing with dark, tiny legs,
To leave couples in feverish fears.

(Mbankolo, 06 January 2013)

Malaria Exported Him

When Anopheles
Injected him with malaria,
He trembled like earth-quaked Haiti

His temperature
Shuttled between 38 and 39.5
And Sanagas flew down his body

His family wealth dwindled
Into ever-pregnant hospital coffers
Leaving members at misery's mercy

Lessons were lost in his class
His office deserted and abandoned
Like a mass graveyard in Syria

His brothers and sisters drew daggers
And scattered into accusation camps
Chasing the very shadows of witchcraft

Finally! Finally, Malaria gathered him
Into a rectangular wooden car
And exported him down to Termiteland

(Mbankolo, 23 April 2013)

Malaria And Fish

Hamadou's family was sleeping without bed nets.
At night, they had mosquitoes for guests.
In the mornings, they had malaria for guests.
Then, Malaria NGOs brought them bed nets.

Hamadou and family were living in the North.
Like fools, they used these nets to catch fish.
Every meal they ate was accompanied by fish
while malaria spread like clouds across the North.

Hamadou's family didn't practice hygiene.
They cared no damn about pools of stagnant water
And would gather like sheep to eat near stagnant water.
Sanitary officials advised them to practice hygiene.

Hamadou and family were living like pigs.
Mosquitoes and germs bred around their compound,
bringing malaria and other diseases to that compound.
And his family started dying like infected pigs.

(Mbankolo, 28 August, 2013)

When Mosquitoes Sing

If the day closes her eyes over your home
and you and your family all snuggle down
into wool-lined beds without mosquito nets,
Anopheles musical bands will come
for nocturnal animation and entertainment.
Singing like Manu Dibango and Grace Decca,
these anophelic band members will land
to rest on the nude parts of your bodies
and drill their mining pipes deep, deep
down into your red liquid ores
in search of blood to fertilize their eggs.
For thank you, they will give you
malaria harbingers to guide and protect
you from sicknesses and untimely deaths.
Soon, the music they sang becomes dirges
sung to accompany your family members to hospitals,
sung to accompany hearses to your home and
sung to accompany corpses to the world beyond.

If darkness spreads his arms over your home
and you and your household all hang up
your bed nets before snuggling down into
the sheets and blankets of your beds,
mosquito musical bands will only hang around
the bed nets and sing for your pleasure
from afar, trapped by the nets each time
they attempt to come closer to your bodies.
The nocturnal, melodious notes from
these anophelic band members will soon
die out in the distance because

they can't land to rest and because
their mining pipes can't reach your blood ores.
Then, they will retire into the mosquito wilderness
in readiness to welcome their own death
while cursing you for their barrenness.
Soon, the music they sang becomes joy anthems
sung to celebrate a Malaria-free World.

(Mbankolo, 29 August, 2013)

Bites of Insanity

In Yaoundé
      Ngong had no nets for mosquitoes
      Yet he lived in very unfriendly ghettos
      Full of ponds of meditating grayish water
      His body's hotness got hotter and hotter
      His head and body began to pain
      He lost his scholarship to Spain

Back in the Village
      Everybody thought him cursed
      Nobody knew he supplied blood barrels
      To colossal colonies of anopheles
      In exchange for billion bites of insanity

Still in Yaoundé
      Ngong divorced with studies, pens and papers
      And began picking plastic papers
      Along Ekounou-Melen streets
      Like a lunatic patient he kept no secrets
      He would line his house with faeces
      And return to it like a pig to pick diseases

Back in the Village
      Everybody agreed Uncle Ndoasak bewitched him
      Nobody knew he still exposed his body
      To colossal colonies of anopheles
      In exchange for billion bites of insanity

In the Village

Ngong came home for rites of tradition
Nobody cared a damn about modern medication
He shuttled between herbalists & diviners for
treatment
Like Chamberlain between Berlin & Paris for
Appeasement
His family wasted away their meagre wealth
In their blind, blind quest for his health

There in the Village
Everybody believed Uncle Ndoasak envied Ngong's
intelligence
Nobody doubted Ba'a Nfo'om's expertise in
necromancy
What links Anopheles to Uncle Ndoasak?
Nothing but bites of insanity

Right in the Village
Ngong finally kicked a bucket
Was wrapped and laid in a wooden pocket
Put into Mother Earth's mouth accompanied by tears
His fiancée and family enveloped in fears
Preparing to send thunder and have killer killed
Can thunder ever have anopheles killed?

Yet in the Village
Everybody thought Uncle Ndoasak a killer
Nobody doubted Ba'a Nfo'om's expertise in
necromancy
What/who really killed Ngong?
Nothing but bites of insanity

(Mbankolo, 01 January 2013)

Printed in the United States
By Bookmasters